PATH OF HOPE

Volume Two:

"Lazarus Speaks"

By R. Darnell Smith

LPP Publishing™

Manchester, CT

PRAY FOR ME

I hope this book

Doesn't find you in vain

With the Lord

I shall remain.

It may seem wrong

In other people's eyes

With him

Still I rise.

So don't fret

Just let things be

If you know the words of prayer

Please pray for me.

.

~ *R. Darnell Smith*

Copyright© 2022 Rickey Darnell Smith

All rights reserved. No part of this book may be reproduced or transmitted in any form or by any means, electronic or mechanical, including photocopying, recording, or by any information storage and retrieval system, without permission in writing from the publisher.

Published by LPP Publishing, Manchester, CT

Lpppublishing1@Gmail.Com

Printed in the United States of America

First paperback edition May 2022

ISBN 978-1-7332643-6-5

CONTENTS

MAN OF THE CLOTH	3
WAKE UP	5
I HAVE DOMINION	7
DO YOU BELIEVE	10
PANIC OR PRAY	11
I WAS PRAYED FOR	13
COUNT YOUR BLESSINGS	15
I COME TO YOU LORD	16
WHY ME?	18
WHY I'M HERE	19
THE ROCK	21
I TRUST THE LORD	22
I THOUGHT I SAW A PROPHET	24
I SAW NOW I SEE	25
THOSE WHO SPITE ME	27
THE SLOTHFUL	28
FOR YOU	30
AIN'T IT GOOD?	31
SOME OF US	33
YOU HEARD	36
YESTERDAY	38

TODAY	41
THIS TIME	43
YOU MUST	45
AN EYE FOR AN EYE & A TOOTH FOR A TOOTH	47
DON'T BLOW IT	50
WORKING CHURCH	52
FAITH	55
FOLLOWING JESUS	57
MY FRIENDS LAWN	59
WHY DO I WRITE?	61
MANNERS	65
THEY SAID I COULDN'T DO IT	67
RUBBISH TO REVIVAL	69
I CAN'T... HE CAN	71
GIVING THANKS	73
LOVE IS LOVE	75
IT'S TIME	76
FAILING FAITH	78
TOXIC	80
ROSES	82

MAN OF THE CLOTH

God gave me life and strength
He made me a man of the cloth
So I must go the length
I must take steps wisely
Choose the right path
God has given life and strength
And I am so glad that he has.

Born leader so I must set the bar
Keep reaching you'll catch a star.
Never giving up
Even when I am tired and weak,
As long as I can talk
Praised scripture I will speak.

Deep down in my heart
I believe he died and rose again,
Upon that time
Is when our journey began.
Even though we're getting up in age
Doesn't mean we can't love him the same.

When things weren't all that good,
We called upon his name
Because we knew that we could
Some call mommy some call daddy
Some even call nephew juice
With the brand new caddy.

Yet he said
Call upon me in times of distress
But many are caught up
In this worldly mess
Putting man before God living through the flesh.

Man of the cloth being anointed
It's your responsibility to teach and lead those
Lost and disappointed.
Bring them back
To they're true calling
Satan got them having a ball
But my Father God got me balling.

WAKE UP

Wake up time is getting near
He said that he would return
Signs and situations shows
He's on his way here.

He told us
About the last days
Look at the famine
The wicked people
And their wicked ways.

Covid we were warned
Are you born again?
Do you believe?
Or will you be scorned?

The weather is unpredictable
Hurricanes tornados
Many major floods
If you believe in anything
I hope it's the blood.

Some are standing still
They have their faith in the stocks
I will definitely let you know
My faith is in the Rock

The sky will break
The winds shall be fierce
They hung him on a cross
His body they did pierce.

Politicians bluntly lying
Tricking one's vote
Do I trust the antichrist?
Nope.

So if your relations
Are not with Jesus Christ
You better get a new outlook
On your life.

Wake up fast time is getting near
Or keep sleeping
When you open your eyes
He'll be here.

I HAVE DOMINION

That serpent is tricky and very slick
Comes in many forms and fashions
But this one was it.
Yet my Father God
Has me convinced
With him by my side
Satan's fire cannot be lit
He's so devious came through the pulpit
The entity spoke in tongues
Like it was a second language.

How this happens I will never know
I thought tongues took over your mouth
And it would just flow.
Not saying I'm right
I may be wrong
Yet this is the first time
I heard tongues being spoken
For ten minutes long.

I no speaketh you English
It all went over my head
We're in the last days
Be careful where you're led.

False prophets' wicked ways are being taught
Some are naive and the fake is being brought.

That serpent is slick and very tricky
So I always keep
My Sword and MY LORD with me.
If it's not social media
Then it's the news
Everywhere you look you see all these dudes.
Pastor Tim, Apostle Greg, Reverend David, and Sister Peg
Everybody ain't going to glory so can you understand the true story.

I don't blame no man for his faults
I chose wrong yet right I thought
So what I did was turn it over to him
I was continuously sinking when I needed to swim.
Again Lucifer has many identities
Comes from all different angles
One mission your brain to get tangled.
All that glitters is not gold
For yourself learn the story so you will know
The real when it's told.
First you say contentment yet you say change is good

Keep up your confusion keep them the way you want them
where you're misunderstood.
God is plain and God is simple
One thing I know he's always with you
Yet the choice is yours if you chose wrong
I suggest all fours.
Get on your knees and fold your hands
Repent for your disobedience then take your stand
Get an understanding of what is called for
When you see or hear Satan shut the door.
Yeah he tried me with his sneaky attack
I guess he didn't know who has my back.

DO YOU BELIEVE

Don't you believe in the Bible?
Do take God's word as an inspired oracle
And as our only guide in living.
Led by the spirit of God I must follow the Bible.

God's will is God's law
We ought to take the teachings of Jesus as vital.
Bear my cross as the Lord Jesus would have me.

God sent me down through the valley of the shadow
The presence of God makes the very surroundings Holy.

Jesus honored the Ten Commandments
And died to satisfy their claims.

Gods blessings is his own presence
Yield my pride and freely follow
The saviors plan the word of God
The kingdom of God.

PANIC OR PRAY

Well

I wanna share with you this

I was lonely distrustful

And I couldn't resist.

In a state of fear

Not knowing which way to turn,

A valuable lesson

I did learn.

I had two choices

On this very day,

It was simple and plain either panic or pray.

My back against the wall heart at a fast rate,

No second guessing or time to hesitate.

I would have two choices on this very day,

It was simple and plain either panic or pray.

I didn't have a mirror yet I found myself in a stare

Little did I know I was in a humble prayer.

Was it my doings? Was it my will?

I felt something soothing. Have you had that feel?

This feeling overwhelmed me left me nothing to say,

Brother man believe me I chose to pray.

In times of distress when you feel you're at your end,
Always remember you can count on him.
Take what little time you have don't have to beg or plead,
When you live righteous with faith he will give all you need.
So here is something I wish and hope you will obey,
In times of turmoil don't panic, just pray.

I WAS PRAYED FOR

I was lost but now I am found,
Satan had me chained and bound.
My world was filled with temptation and lust,
Only in the getting over I did trust.
I use to judge claiming what I saw,
By any means I would break the law.
Well someone was praying because I sure wasn't,
Ask the Lord for something come on cousin.
I ran I hid did all I could to flee,
Again someone prayed for me.
Moms always said "I 'ma pray for you boy"
I heard it so much I never knew it brought her joy.
Okay let's get to the matter,
Without those prayers I know I couldn't have the,
Relation I have with the great I AM,
He's always knew me and had his own plan.
On days when I just plum given up,
He would then overflow my cup.
So at this time I would like to give praise,
To God almighty for his merciful ways.

See plenty claim his favor for the wrong reasons,
Do they understand blessings come always
Not in certain seasons?
But you must definitely put in some work to get ahead,
How is it stated faith without works is dead.

___COUNT YOUR BLESSINGS___

Count your blessings as you walk closer to thee,
Let the Holy Spirit set you free.
Give praise for overcoming hard times that you came against,
Remember the joy of the Lord is your strength.
You may have sinned and lived very trife,
You don't have to live that way anymore
Let God change your life.
Don't stand in rebellion and take thing for granted,
Your one of his seeds so bloom where you're planted.
Through the graciousness of God the four runner of Christ,
Let the Trinity move all through your life.
Some may smirk and say this is odd,
But never forget you were born in the image of God.

I COME TO YOU LORD

To you Lord I come humble,

I did falter, yes I did stumble.

Through your mercy I did suffer,

You and only you made my trails tougher

Deny your word I put it on hold

I simply forgot how your story was told.

This world offers many different things,

When I should only accept what the good Lord brings.

Well I settled for the wrong possessions,

Which left me stuck with no progressions.

Being caught up in the flesh meaning to sin,

Forgetting the fact you gave me a win.

If I listen and follow you teaching,

The sky's the limit so I will keep reaching.

When I say reaching there are a few steps

Repentance and prayer and a whole lot of reps.

Let go and let God it is all written,

Slow down relax and start sittin'

This may sound weird but you better get in line,

One thing I know he's always on time.

To you Lord yes I come humble,
I did falter I did stumble it's fourth and goal
I cannot fumble.
I am going to score I am breaking the plain,
Through my faith and obedience in God's name.

WHY ME?

I wonder sometimes why me?
WHY NOT ME.
Influenced and blinded I couldn't see,
Through faith I've learned it was destined to be.
Many times I've looked in the wrong direction,
Turning to my family and spouse for protection.
They both lead me to one common device,
Turn my total life over to Christ.
I said I would and played with Church,
But did the street thing thought it wouldn't hurt.
Little did I know there was a plan,
Whatever it took I would understand.
I may be confined within this fence,
Now everything is making some sense.
Through all that time I was misled,
If I wasn't here would I be dead.
I wonder sometimes why me?
Influenced and blinded I couldn't see
Through faith I've learned it was destined to be.

WHY I'M HERE

Satan the beast,
For your soul he's out to steal,
If you're not Born Again,
He'll show you Hell is real.
Have you found Salvation?
In Jesus your Savior?
There's life in the Blood,
Listen let me tell ya.
Without Christ,
You don't stand a chance,
When sin catches up with you,
With the Devil you'll dance.

I am not here to hate,
Like those who expired,
Those without Faith,
All burned in the Lake of Fire.
Sin separates us from God
And that's too much for me to bare
To obey the Word of God,
This is why I am here.

First I thought I was cursed,
And left in a place of hate,
Now I know I am here,
To get myself straight.
So while I am here,
I must forget about my pride,
And gain knowledge wisdom and understanding,
From deep inside.

I must release those Demons,
I use to possess,
Give one hundred percent to God,
And nothing less.
Half my heart that won't be enough,
Giving my all makes it easy,
When times get rough.
I will listen close,
To my Holy Visitation,
And turn to God to help build a new nation.

THE ROCK

How can I,
Put blame on man,
When my foundation,
Is built on sand.
I need to get,
My life on lock,
Must build my foundation,
On the Rock.
My plans and thoughts,
Were all mine,
I simply thought,
It would be fine.
Here is something,
Which should be herd,
Solid foundations consist,
Of obeying God's word.
Hearing God's word,
Is what it be,
Living and doing his word,
Is the key.
Well I must listen,
Take action live my life on lock,
Build my foundation,
On the MIGHTY ROCK.

I TRUST THE LORD

I trust the lord,

With all my heart,

Now it's time,

I do my part.

Repent for my sins,

And praise his name,

His light will guide me,

Down the eternal lane.

Some may disbelieve,

And not have faith,

He offers himself as a gift,

Get yourself straight.

Except he is all,

That you will need

Then take the dip,

And follow his lead.

Change doesn't happen,

In an instant

So pray with diligence,

And stay persistent.

Old friends will hate,

But you must rebuke,

Knowing within his name,

There is nothing but truth.

Don't take it from me,
Gain knowledge for self,
Just trust in his name,
You'll need nothing else.
Forgive me father,
For I have sinned,
Not just once,
But again and again.
Through your name,
I believe you will forgive,
So I may move on with my life,
And eternally live.
If you are unconvinced,
That Christ is all he claimed to be,
Give him your life,
And live sin free.
Now your gonna face choices,
Time to choose on your own,
But always remember,
Who sits on the throne.
If you made a decision,
To put your trust in Christ,
Then you did a good job,
So enjoy your life.

I THOUGHT I SAW A PROPHET

In my days of youth I was misled,

I should have listened to the things you said.

Service every Sunday we would attend,

Then and there is where it began.

I was on the right track had faith and belief,

Until I got older and learned the streets.

Wow the fast lane I just couldn't stop it

Then and there I thought I saw a profit.

My mind was trapped spirits were confused,

The takeover of my soul left me abused.

Following the way of those I thought would win,

Blinded to the fact I was buried within sin.

The word to me had no meaning,

I only believed in the fast money scheming.

The women and drugs that life I couldn't stop it,

Still I thought I saw a profit.

Through all this sin there came a time,

When problems left me in a bind.

Now all it did was prove to me this,

The profit I saw never really exist.

Within my sight was the Devils device,

Which blinded from the real PROPHET,

Who works for CHRIST.

I SAW NOW I SEE

I've seen a lot of right and a whole lot of wrong,
It's something like the same ole song.
But do you understand it's all top forty,
It's what the people request you herd you shorty.
So don't go placing the blame solely on the flesh,
You had a choice in your mess.
You made a mistake admit and move on,
God's mercy forgives from dusk till dawn.
Now don't think you can just receive,
You must have faith and also believe.
A lot of folk joke and play foolish games,
Thinking they can repent and still remain.
Well the Lord knows if your repentance is real,
Or are you out for blessings to steal.
When things don't simply go your way,
The Lord knows you were out just to play.
So know your game the rules and the score,
If you're not giving your all then give some more.
The rules are made the clock is ticking,
Get yourself right and please stop slipping.
You can't always be placing the blame,
When you lose in this here game.

You're not the coach owner or G.M.

Only one has three authorities and that one is him.

For those who do not know who this may be,

Read the WORD, know the WORD then you will see.

THOSE WHO SPITE ME

Lord forgive those who spite me, for the do not know,
Through their spitefulness, my spirit grows.
Those who claim through vain they hurt me,
Little do they know they help me spiritually
Well I have learned through setbacks I learn,
That God helps my attitude, this is his concern.
So while the haters keep on with the way they hate,
I know that they're not in my fate.
I will put it like this for all them to except,
I love your hatred yet I won't neglect.
The reason you dislike my walk with my head up,
Simply because your life is all messed up.
Not pointing any fingers or calling any names,
But I really hope you don't go insane.
As you see your wickedness only gives me pride,
So do what you do. I am open wide.
Next time you think you're holding me back,
Learn about my Salvation,
Can you get with that?
I love my brothers as I love myself,
I can only be judged by the Lord and nobody else.

THE SLOTHFUL

A closed mouth doesn't get fed,

Ask and you shall receive is how it is read.

A lazy man gains nothing through his ways,

Yet these are the ones who constantly complain.

Well to those should I show compassion?

Or should I punch the gas and keep on mashing.

Do they understand you don't work you don't eat,

Still they expect the hard worker to kiss their feet.

As I live my life abiding by the Word,

I will let the lazy one sit on a log like a turd.

Different times I break down and give some Mercy,

Only praying one day that they will be worthy.

I cannot make no man get off his rear,

I can only put a little something in his ear.

Definitely I hope they listen and change,

Their whole life they rearrange.

I tell them take it from me I was once like you,

Depending on others to do what I was supposed to do.

Until I got introduced to my spirituality,

And started living my life in reality.

Man this life is so much better,

Ever since I got my life together.

Again a closed mouth doesn't get fed,

But you can eat through the knowledge that's read.

Get up get out and go get something,

Get off your rear or settle for nothing.

FOR YOU

For you my Lord I live and I breathe,

For you my Lord my heart does receive.

The love emotions tranquility and remorse,

But the wicked world offers evil to break my course.

You know these attributes which will take you under,

It all looks good, even the rain and thunder.

Before I accepted your mercy and grace,

I just traveled in circles at a steady pace.

Me chasing my tail it all got old,

I leaned on the Rock and my hands I did fold.

I opened the Sword and learned the truth,

I was changed like Clark Kent in the phone booth.

But you're the real Superman,

I am super too, as I follow your command.

For you Lord I breathe and I live,

For you my heart receives all what you did.

So as I continue on my new found travels,

I'll lean on the Mighty Rock and come out of the gravel.

AIN'T IT GOOD?

Don't be carnal, or a professional sinner,
Satan is creeping,
Hear him and obey him,
Wake up and stop sleeping.
A word from God
"COME TO ME AS A MAN AND I WILL HELP",
"I WANT TO BRING MERCY TO THOSE THROUGH THE HOLY SPIRIT FELT".
Life is an obstacle course,
So what you're gonna do,
Give a little more,
Be a living Epistle,
God is dealing with you.
Don't miss the flight,
God speaks perfectly
Be honest,
Take responsibility.
Hide and he can't help,
Are you ever gonna change?
Give him time to get you ready,

You're praying,

But not waiting for him to rearrange.

The time is now,

So answer to Christ,

I answered,

And he saved my life.

SOME OF US

Why do some take kindness for weakness?
It's use or be used,
While in my youth
I mastered these rules.
I am grown now
And the game remains the same,
But through my trials and tribulations
I have changed.
While I've changed
The world keeps spinning,
I shall seek my Salvation
In this life filled with sinning.
Judge
He said "vengeance is mines",
He also said "he who holds his tongue is wise".
Back to the flesh
Those not anointed,
While you point one finger
Four others are pointed.
Those without sin
Cast the first stone,

I shouldn't be throwing rocks
All alone.
Sin is in our nature
So pray and repent,
For our fathers forgiveness
It doesn't cost a cent.
Some say pay the storehouse
You know your tides,
But what if I have no income,
Will they let me ride?
Hypocritical missionaries putting gas on the fire,
Are the first ones
Wanting solos in the choir.
Bible study
Your opinion is your own,
Learn something
Your reaps already sewn.
The righteous one
Takes note of the house of the wicked
And brings the wicked to ruin,
Rich and poor have this in common,
The Lord is the maker of them all

So do you know what you're doing?
So I will end this poem
Written for those who use
And take kindness for a weakness
To their brother,
When God ends your days
You'll never see another.

YOU HEARD

Lord help me
As I struggle once again,
The flesh has deceived me
Now Satan claims a win.
You know I know better
So my knees shall bend,
I'll repent, I'll confess,
Just keep me away from him.
Jesus cleanse me
For I have kept the faith,
Always knowing from the devil
You would help me escape.
In a fight I was
But the war isn't mine,
So I will be a winner
Through your grace divine.
So I must change the way I live
By changing the way I think,
To be someone I never was
Is the missing link.
My transformation consists
Of being a savior and a spiritual leader,
Before this transformation
I was neither.

The war isn't mine

So in this fight I will not run,

I will end this poem

With Psalms chapter 131 verse 1 *(GNT: Good News Translation)*

"LORD I HAVE GIVEN UP MY PRIDE AND TURNED AWAY FROM MY ARROGANCE.
I AM NOT CONCERNED WITH GREAT MATTERS OR WITH SUBJECTS TOO DIFFICULT FOR ME"

YESTERDAY

Yesterday is gone

Yet I will continue,

What's next?

"Um"

Let me check the menu.

We got some prayer, praise,

Worship and devotion,

It all looks good,

Another journey in motion.

You know I can't chose,

They all need to be done,

Like those Lay's potato chips,

You can't have just one.

As I take my daily doses,

Of all those good things,

It's something like Mary Mary,

Boy can they sing.

My prayers are answered

Through obedience and faith,

But I also must repent

For all my mistakes.

I give praise
For a new love found,
Because when praises go up
Blessings come down.
I worship with force
And a whole lot of spirit,
Got ole Lucifer timid
My beliefs he fears it.
Devotion yeah
"I am truly devoted",
I study the Word regularly
Many verses get quoted.
Yesterday is gone
Today is right here,
For all those lost souls
I'll continue with prayer.
Again
My prayers are being answered
These days,
I've even led a few non-believers
Into praise.

Now with devotion and worship

They come along,

Looking for tomorrow,

Because yesterday is gone,

TODAY

Today I rose
Through the grace of Christ,
It may be raining,
Still I love my life.
It says after the sunshine
Comes the rain,
See through my faith and obedience
I will maintain.
The world may be in deep transition,
This is why I give praise with joy
And keep on my mission.
Well
You must take the good
Along with the bad,
I thank God Almighty,
Jesus is someone I have.
That Lucifer hates
On those who believe,
He will test your faith
With lust,
He's out to deceive.

Now say your prayers,

Give devotion and praise,

You'll still have good comings,

On those bad days.

The pain, grief,

Sunshine and rain,

I will count it all as joy,

In his name.

As the day settles,

And the sun starts to drop,

I thank God, for giving his only begotten Son,

The only way to the top.

If you don't know the Son,

You can't know the Father,

Either follow directions,

Or don't even bother.

So as days pass

And your mind is still twisted,

Unravel those kinks fast,

Or you be done missed it.

Today I rose

Through the grace of Christ,

And I will rise after death,

For eternal life.

THIS TIME

Hesitant never, competition none,
I shall never again put myself
Before, God's son.
"Why do you call me Lord, Lord
And do not do the things which I say?"
If you love me, keep my commandments,
Meaning obey.
I use to think I was perfect,
Thought I had equal value,
My profound importance,
Led me to not have you.
I must reluctantly relinquish self-compassion,
My worthless goal,
Paul said
"If you think you are standing firm
You had better be careful
That you do not fall".
This time thy Word is truth,
So thy Word must come first,
I am tired of living in darkness,
And dying of thirst.
I wanna live in the light,
Destroy old habits,
It's out there waiting,

I must grab it.

This world offers a great deal of sin,

I mean you must have faith,

And believe within.

Change is a mainstay,

That must be acquired,

From the world to God,

It's what's desired.

Sanctify, separate, you know,

Kick it to the curb,

These things of the world,

You and I don't deserve.

So this time,

I shall use my mental and physical,

To follow his directions,

Instead of the worldly

Do what it do.

I will use thy Word because it is true,

And then this time,

I will let thy Word,

Do what it do.

YOU MUST

As the earth continues to rotate,

On its axis,

There are two things you must do,

Die and pay taxes.

Well one,

You may can avoid,

But the other,

Some grieved,

While others enjoyed.

See when your number is called,

Which direction will you go?

If you don't,

I think you should know.

All it takes is faith and belief,

For those who are lost,

Listen to this speech.

(ROMANS 10 verses 9 and 10)

That if you confess with your mouth, "Jesus is Lord",

And believe in your heart that God raised him from the dead, you will be saved.

For it is with your heart that you believe and are justified,

And it is with your mouth that you confess and are saved.

Now if this catches you,

And throws you overboard,

Read the mighty words,

Written in the sword.

As you read,

You must understand,

These stories are about,

One great man.

He's the first and the last,

The truth and the life,

If you don't get it the first time,

Then you should read it twice.

We'll all I can do is say,

"Take it from me",

"I pay my taxes",

"And heavens where I'll be".

AN EYE FOR AN EYE & A TOOTH FOR A TOOTH

An eye for an eye

And a tooth for a tooth,

That was my way of growing

As a youth.

I use to believe

This was stern and good,

You couldn't show no weakness

In my hood.

I mean things would happen,

You better show no slack,

I even heard a few parents say

You better hit them back.

Funny thing

The cartoons promoted violence,

Is this why

Children practice defiance.

If you take a look around,

Many kids are hateful,

By the notches in your belt

Is how they rate you.

An eye for an eye

And a tooth for a tooth,

You can't gangbang,

If you're not hundred proof.

I got older

Did a little changing

I got wise,

I chose my friends different

Only hung with certain guys.

That fighting mentality

Soon started to dwindle,

Picked up on something new,

Learned to swindle.

You see a good talk game,

Could be just as severe,

The right words put together,

Could cause fear.

Wickedness done

Either mental or physical,

Both hinder your walk

When you wanna walk spiritual.

See an eye for an eye

And a tooth for a tooth,

I don't spread that message

To my youth.

But I will tell them,

Don't be no punk,

This don't mean
Go starting junk.
So if someone strikes you
Defend yourself,
Always protect
Your wealth and your health.
Depending on how you live,
Is how you handle the truth,
Will it be
An eye for an eye
Or a tooth for a tooth?

DON'T BLOW IT

Each day
There is some type of force,
Trying to knock me
Off my righteous course.
Through the grace of God
I've found Christ today,
With all my heart
I've acknowledged him
In all my ways.
I'm like the mind of an elephant
With my faith,
Always remembering
He'll keep my path straight.
He's a sustainer
You can't do it on your own,
Next to God he's set high,
On a throne.
He came into a world
Unfit for his royalty,
Now all we must give
Is our loyalty.

In content and hard to please
That's not how it should be,
Must Jesus bear the cross alone
And all the people go free.
Have room for Jesus
To come in your life and change,
Don't take the differences that occur
To be all that strange.
To serve Jesus
Is a fight with the flesh,
Or should I say Satan
Putting you through a test.
So don't blow your stack,
Keep your head straight and level,
Because God will help us
Withstand the wilds of the Devil.

WORKING CHURCH

Good morning all

In the house of the Lord,

I pray you have on your armor

And are clutching your sword,

Defiance is something

We cannot afford.

Yes he's merciful

He do forgives,

But are you ready to change

The way in which you live?

See some come in shame

Totally out of fear,

These are the ones

I am grateful they are here.

Others practice persistence

Claiming their own pew,

Be careful,

He knows what you do,

Yet you still wonder

What's happening with you

I call them

Sunday saints

Here for church service,

Yet service they can't.

I won't call no names,

I ain't gone put you out there,

It's not for me to judge,

But I do care.

Have you ever sat and wondered

Took a second glance,

Things just don't happen,

Simply by chance.

Faith in the unseen

Man it is terrific,

It's a whole lot better

Than a scratch ticket.

Let me get back

To something we all should hoard,

"Yeah"

I am talking about

The house of the Lord.

This message here

Is for all those salvation achievers

Ones who are part

Of a local body of believers.

For those appointed pastors,

Still serving the Lord

Every time I see them

In their hands is a sword.

Be Careful

Some are trying,

Just to get ahead,

To the seven churches of Revelation

To whom Jesus said,

"I KNOW YOUR WORKS"

So to the martyrs

I know this really hurts.

But boy I am proud to be a member,

Of a working church.

FAITH

I am expressing thoughts
Through my anointed pen,
These thoughts are those
That arose through sin.
Sometimes I write
With no direction,
The ink just flows
With the Holy Spirit as protection.
So bear with me
And take this ride,
With my anointed pen
And Christ as the guide.
Don't get me wrong
I do play my part,
By simply letting Christ
Control my heart.
He oversees
My daily routine,
By keeping my emotions high
And my spirits clean.
I'm expressing thoughts
Thoughts through my anointed pen,
These thoughts are those,
That arose through sin.

My mind comes and sometimes goes,

Through these actions,

My knowledge of God grows.

In my life I've been here and there,

Never was I scared

Or had much fear.

Little did I know

Who controlled my fate,

But through the Word of God

I am happy to state,

That God is good

And God is great,

And through his understanding,

I can hold my weight.

Again expressing thoughts

Through my anointed pen,

Helps me rebuke Satan

And a life of sin

And it gives me a spot

In the Lambs book of Life where my name is in.

FOLLOWING JESUS

Living it up
Through his Grace,
What was
Is no longer
In my face.
Memories keeps
Many depressed,
Foolishness
Let go of that mess.
We don't know no better
Please don't settle,
Stop placing the blame
On others living in the ghetto.
Stay focused
Through your walk of faith,
Make a stand
Before you reach that gate.
Who you think you fooling
It's either break or get broken,
Follow the light
Keep it movin'
Trust in the Lord
Not in the flesh,
Trust in the Lord

Forget the rest.
He said "acknowledge me
In all my ways.
Feel the Lord and apart from evil,
So what
If they don't believe you?
Stop looking
In the wrong places,
Everyone's pushing dreams
God already knows,
It's only manifested
Through their faces.
Seeking the living
Through the dead,
God is the real deal,
Did you hear what I said?
God will
So let go and let God,
He said
"Pick up your cross and follow me,
That's your job.
Stay close
You can't fall behind
He can have your flesh,
But your soul is mine.

MY FRIENDS LAWN

I have a friend I like to go visit, her lawn there is so green and plush. There are a lot of statues, old and new that I like to see. She would tell me of her woes, I would listen so intently. We had our good times, most even great. I shared her sadness when she cried… and cheered her when she was depressed. She counts on me and I counted on her. I go now to lay on her green plush lawn and talk to her statue, where she lays peacefully down below.

Many think the Devil
Claimed her
In her last days of life,
Do they know?
She was right with Christ.
This is why
I visit my friend on her lawn,
I go by and see her,
When it's quiet - around dawn.
We've had many memories
Good and bad,
I really know
She wouldn't want me to be sad.

She's better now
Much less pain,
So I will handle myself
I must maintain.
To go to her lawn
And chat with her statue,
Out of all my things daily,
It's the best thing I do.
I listen
With an intense mind frame,
She tells me
Things are not the same.
There are a lot of others
To keep her occupied,
I show up and show her
I am still by her side.
While earthly beings
Think she's down in the dirt,
I will not let
My feelings get hurt.
It's simply like
Taking my medication,
The prescription prescribed
Is daily meditation.

WHY DO I WRITE?

Why do I write some say I am lonely,
I would rather talk to you than some homie.
Homie got me twisted in this worldly condition,
Side tracked from my spiritual mission.
I know my job is to reach and teach,
But homie got no time for me to preach.
The world offers fun and excitement,
The world offers joy and enlightenment.

I tried one day to explain the Blood,
The homie said "I'm a Crip… what up cuz".
He thought I had fear and pulled out a gun,
Then he looked puzzled when I did not run.
I said "The Blood not no gang",
"My turf is the church, that's where I hang".

I said "when you die where your gonna go',
He said "six feet deep don't you know'.
I said "well I'm going to eternal life",
"Where everything is so nice".
He said "hold up how you know",
I said "in this lifetime I let my spirit grow".
"Faith" I said "yeah I do believe",
"My salvation I will receive".

He looked kinda shocked like some game I was running,
At the same time his peoples were coming.
So I told him I would get with him on another date,
He said "yeah I want some more on that fait".
I told him its faith and not fate,
I gave him a time and said don't be late.

He remembered the time and the place,
Funny thing he had this look on his face.
So I asked him what's with that expression,
He said "listen my brother I have a confession".
"As a youngster I attended service on the regular",
"I was in contention to be a great competitor".
"My dad was deacon moms sang in the choir",
"Working towards salvation was their desire".
"Until one day it was a terrible wreck",
"Mom was thrown from the car, Dad broke his neck".
"I cried day in and day out",
"I've lost both parents I began to shout".
"God what have I done",
"Why did you leave me a parentless son?"
"From that point I didn't see no reason,
"Service never came, I had no season".
"I went out in the world',

"Got caught with drugs money and jezebel",
"That fast girl".
"I found pleasure in all this sin",
"That's where my wicked life got its begin".
"You know at this point I am getting tired",
"But I wonder one thing",
"Did they find salvation before they expired?"
"I really miss them this is no debate",
"So I would like to learn more about this fait".
I then let him know its faith not fate,
And reassured him it wasn't too late.
I spoke to him on how he could join them again,
Through meditating and following Romans 10 verses 9 & 10.
So I gave him a sword and showed him where,
I told through belief and faith he could be there.

He took the word no time he was wasting,
He said "I have faith in my salvation".
I said "hold up wait a minute my friend",
"You also have to be born again".
"Born again what do you mean?"
"You must wash away your sins",
"Become clean".
Give your life to Christ surrender to the boss,
Put down your gun and pick up your cross.

Love thy brother as you love yourself,
Put God first and nobody else.
He looked at me and replied,
"Yeah I'll do it",
From the look on his face I really knew it.
He went on his way sword in hand,
Head held high with a new plan.
I seen him around two weeks later,
He said to me "there's no one greater".
As a looked into his eyes I could see this glow,
Before he said another word,
I said "I already know".

Some say I am lonely that's the reason I write,
They don't understand that I follow the light,
And as long as it is bright I will continue to write.

MANNERS

Honor thy father and mother,
So your days will be longer.
Do some really understand?
This is what makes the family bond stronger.

As kids you do childish things,
As you mature those ways must disappear,
You must gain respect for others,
And learn how to care.

Yet you have grown folks carry on like infants,
They look around and don't know,
Where the time went.

Trapped up in the world the hustle and the bustle,
They end up like Sampson, when he cut his hair,
No muscle.

Ye with no sin cast the first stone,
When I was a kid,
I would have been the first one,
Who would have thrown.

This is why I thank Father God,
For keeping me until I was grown.
At times I didn't honor my mother or my dad,
Also at times I was grateful that I had.

For this reason our bond is much stronger,
I love the fact
My days are much longer.

THEY SAID I COULDN'T DO IT

They said

I couldn't do it

I begged the differ,

Through my trials and tribulations

My strength in the Lord

Got a whole lot stiffer.

It was not

An easy journey,

I praise his name

Because he is worthy.

I worship Father God

With continued faith,

I thank Father God now,

Even when

I've made a mistake.

They said

That I couldn't do it,

At times this set me back,

I was lost and confused

Running with the pack.

Through prayer and repentance,

I came out of the darkness,

I am on my way

To spiritual fitness.

Anything you want
You must work hard to achieve,
Caught in my worldly ways
I did not believe.
Yet God had his way,
My transformation continues,
Prayer repentance
And worship stays on my menu.
They said
I couldn't do it,
I guess they were right,
I didn't do it
He did it,
And I am not afraid to recite.
So to all the naysayers,
Those not affiliated,
I will let them know,
If I would have kept trying on my own,
I would never have made it.

RUBBISH TO REVIVAL

Stand on God's word

Lord Lord

You are my strength,

Hell is real

It's not a myth,

Those pearly gates,

My focus is straight,

As I travel the length.

When I see Peter

Not looking for the hook up,

My life I gave to you,

My name is in the Lambs Book of life,

Flip the pages, just look it up.

I cleaned my rubbish

Changed my views,

Simple and plain

I left my life to you.

I wanna go see the Lord,

And upon my arrival,

You will see I turned,

My rubbish to revival.

As we meet and settle the score,

When I leave this world,

To return no more.

See
I am going
To be with my friend,
Let the redeemed of the Lord
Say amen.

I CAN'T... HE CAN

When I try to accomplish,

Things out of reach,

I surrender to his will,

The lessons he teaches.

Lean not,

To my understanding,

Leaning on the Rock,

This keeps me standing.

True I may fall,

My scuffs and bruises,

Trials and tribulations,

The tools that he uses.

When you stray from your maker,

Not following his path,

Things do get drastic,

When he cast down his wrath.

I can't,

Yet I know he can,

So I seek refuge,

I follow his plan.

This may sound difficult,

So don't get upset and pout,

Pray with remorse,

Just stay on his route.

These four words,

Should be in high demand,

Yet always remember,

I CAN'T… HE CAN.

GIVING THANKS

Giving thanks first,
As I open my eyes
Through my faith and belief
Another day I rise.
Father God
Your Mercy endureth forever
It may rain may storm
I am ready for whatever.
You see you must take the good and the bad
Your ups and your downs
I can only deal with it
Because I keep you around
I remember times
When I backslid
I ducked and dodged
Ran and I hid.
Seeking worldly things
Caught up in the flesh
I thought I was living good
Didn't see the mess.
That Devil has a plan and he's very slick,
He'll have you thinking your living healthy
Yet all the while you're sick.
I will admit I was lost in the sauce

Daily working hard

For the wrong boss

I was so wicked that I got fired

I guess someone was praying for me

Because without applying I got hired

My time with that Devil had expired

I guess you knew I was lost in the sauce

Yes I guessed

Yet you knew you were the boss

I am here to tell you

It's never too late

He's a forgiving God

So get yourself straight

He did it for me

And I know he will

Do it for you

The door is always open

You must just come through

Giving thanks first

As I open my eyes

And giving me strength

Each day I rise.

LOVE IS LOVE

Who shall come between my union?
No money no car no home or human
No Covid no Katarina war or politician

For the scribes present
We as pawns in the game
Prepared for our duty

Through all the turmoil
His mercy endures forever

In confidence I know
Idols Demons Ghost or Spirits
Neither here nor there.

How high or low any type of beast
Shall come between my union
The love of God which is in Christ.

IT'S TIME

Are you ready

For the Father to return?

have you applied yourself?

His mercy did you earn?

From your bad decisions

A lesson did you learn?

Do you understand purpose?

Yes you have one

Remember God gave

His only begotten son

Churches are filled

With people seeking change

Many believers

Are tired of doing the same thang

You are not alone

You can't rub it off

The Holy Ghost is here

To rescue the lost

Let the process make me holy

Bring me out of a life

Filled with turmoil

Bring me into God's kingdom

With the rich soil

God gives you choice
And I hope you chose wise
Keep your heart wide open
To accept the prize
Life after death eternal living
He's the master
Of gift giving
To my brother and my sister
Who lives in a bind
I am here to tell you
It's that time
So put your faith in him
You have to stop running
He said he shall return
And yes he is coming
So if you are looking
I know you can find
Do you hear those trumpets?
Yes it's time.

FAILING FAITH

Do you believe
He died for our sins?
Are you tired of living life
With no wins?
you may know the story
and have a clue
Yet are you stuck on Jesus
Like gorilla glue?
Do you know you must
Put in hard work?
You must do service
Not just attend church
Help your neighbor
In your hood volunteer
God would never put upon you
What you could not bare
Failing faith
Meaning waiting on results
You have to go out
And it put your laziness
On halt
Faith without works is dead
It also say
A closed mouth doesn't get fed

God has a plan for me

And it's not worldly it's wordly

And by faith

I can be set free

Everybody won't make it

So you better get right

Keep your focus clear

Keep God in your sight

Walk with faith

Stay in the system

March your body of faith

Keep it in rhythm

How you're going to get to heaven

When while on earth

You can't follow the assignment

Failing faith is not

Part of the movement

Being prepared

Is most important.

TOXIC

You have some people
Who are never satisfied
They complain and nothing's
Ever to their satisfaction
Well I've been thinking
And came up with this thesis
The answer I came up with is
They need Jesus
I mean the sun will be shining
And a very cool breeze
Yet they will find something wrong
With the sway of the trees
A clear night sky
With all the stars in line
They will still point out something
Wrong in their view
They just have to wine
Out for dinner with family and friends
Yet the service from the waiter is wrong
When will this end

The bread was cold
The meal wasn't up to par
The ranking of the restaurant
Was full five star
When I go around people like this
I use to get mad and not have fun
Until I learned why God gave
His begotten son
Everyone is one of his children
Yet some tend to leave us
Those are the ones I know
Who needs Jesus
If you ever come across someone
Living in a state of just can't get right
Do me a favor
Turn on God's light
Try to open their eyes
To this wonderful sight
If you must tell them
About my thesis
Point them in the right direction
Send them to Jesus.

ROSES

Give them their roses

While they are still hear

You would never know

When their time is near

If you have disputes

That have not yet been solved

When they're gone

You will feel like

You were robbed

Your family friends

Even work people

Put your pride aside

Come clean

Make things equal

God giveth

And he can taketh away

Tell them you love them

Each and every day

You never forgave the drug addict

Who stole from you when you were friends

Life's too short
Make amends
Give them their roses
When they are still around
Simply because
They won't see them
When they're in the ground.

www.ingramcontent.com/pod-product-compliance
Lightning Source LLC
Chambersburg PA
CBHW060347050426
42449CB00011B/2855